Through My Eyes
Poetry About My Life

Charity Aschenbrener

Thank you to everyone who inspired me and helped me through everything. You know who you are. I love you guys.

Cupid's Chokehold

"You've got that smile that only heaven can make, I pray to God everyday to keep you forever." –Chris Brown

Amber Rose

You said that I was perfect,
I was your bride-to-be.
Tell me you still mean that,
You're only gone temporarily.

Tell me that you love me
And in a few years you'll be back.
We had something, call it love,
And I know we proved that.

You always made me smile
Even when I was in tears.
We loved for several months,
But it felt like several years.

Two kids. One love.
That was strong and true.
There is only one man for me
And that man is you.

Whether it takes a few months,
A year, or even two.
I'll be here waiting,
Waiting for you.

I promised I'd always love you.
I promised I'd never leave,
That's what I plan to do.
You're the oxygen I breathe.

28 months. So far away.
True love never dies, so baby I will wait.
Meeting you was a gift of chance.
But falling in love with you was fate.

Baby, You Are My Dream

I never said love would be easy
I know that we'd really have to try
I'll do everything I can to keep you
And here is the reason why:
I'd give everything and anything
But I won't ever give up.

Ballad of Love

Once upon a time,
Not too long ago
I came upon boy in love
With a girl white as snow.
She loved him
With her whole heart
I wonder if he felt the same
From the very start?
Things happen for a reason
Sometimes a reason we don't know,
But if it's meant to be it will happen,
If it's not, let it go.
The girl introduced us
She was my friend
And since the moment he & I met
I wanted to be with him until the end.
I hid my feelings very well
I did my best not to let the show
After a few encounters
He let his own feelings known.
Things happen for a reason
Sometimes a reason we don't know,
But if it's meant to be it will happen,
If it's not, let it go.
He told me of a connection
He felt when looking in my eyes
And then he pulled me close
As his lips met mine.
That kiss…Was the beginning
Of a love meant to be.
He told her goodbye
And then he came to me.
Things happen for a reason
Sometimes a reason we don't know,
But if it's meant to be it will happen,
If it's not, let it go.
A love that isn't perfect
But it's a love that's true.
This is the story entitled
The Story of Me and You.

Besame. Abrazame. Amame.

I trust you with my tears
And my secrets never told.
I trust you with my hopes and fears,
And this hand to hold.
I know you'll be true
Whenever we're apart.
I trust you.
I trust you with my heart.

I've held back so long,
Not wanting to give it all.
Looking for a place to land,
Not wanting to fall.
You showed me how to give.
You let me take my time.
You said one day it will work
I'll be yours and you'll be mine.

Bye.!

To get it right.
To get it wrong.
To break up &
Come back strong.

You do it for the money.
You do it for the show.
It's done with pleasure
Cause you know you get the dough.

We get in a fight.
You lie to my face.
I'll put you out of my mind.
Without a single trace

I'll kill your rep.
I'll spit on your name.
I'm the player &
You're the game.

When I hugged you
You got goosebumps on your skin
Baby it was only a game
That you could never win.

I'm Not A Perfect Person

What happened to forever?
What happened to no goodbye?
What happened to not giving up
And how we'd always try?

What happened to forever?
What happened to true love?
What to me being the girl
That you've been dreaming of?

What happened to forever?
What happened to you and I?
What happened to being together
Until the day we die?

What happened to forever?
What happened to always?
What happened to the connection
We had those summer days?

What happened to forever?
What happened to me and you?
What happened to the promise
That we'd always make it through?

What happened to forever?
What happened to no other?
What happened to the days
You used to call me your lover?

What happened to forever?
What happened to "your girl"?
What happened to me
Meaning more than the world?

What happened to forever?
What happened to "I swear"?
What happened to no matter what
You would always be there?

What happened to forever?
What happened to you and me?
What happened to the promise
That we'd always be?

Forever is still possible
And you proved to me it is.
You came back you with
An "I love you" and a kiss.

I Will Hold You Up

I know that I'm not perfect,
Because no one in this world can be.
But you're the closest thing to perfect,
Because that's what you are to me.
The tears fall steadily from your eyes
And you're so far away
I can't wait until you get home
I'm counting down the days.
We've had our ups and downs
And I know there are more to come
But I'll always be by your side
And when all is said and done
I'll hold your hand
And catch you when you fall.
I'll be there to support you.
I'll be our brick wall.
There's one thing I have to say
And believe me, it is true
It may sound a bit cliché
But I truly do love you.

Like Me

Only fools like me can write poems so true.
Only God can give me an angel, as beautiful as you.

Only I can make up these silly rhymes.
But only God can make you mine.

Living Life

When I die
I want it to be like this
My last conscience memory
Is our last kiss.

I want you
To be the last thing I see
Whether it be awake
Or while I'm asleep.

I want to leave
While I'm curled in your arms.
While I'm fast asleep
And you're keeping me from harm.

Or while I'm awake
Holding your hand
Or maybe in a meadow.
Or in water? Or sand?

I want a peaceful ending
And I want it quiet too
I don't want to be alone
I want to die with you.

Louis Vuitton

I'm so happy that you're back.
That once again you're mine.
You're all I want, all I need.
You're always on my mind.

I love you so much
Even when we're apart.
I never gave up on us
You've always had my heart.

Through sickness and in health.
Whether we're rich or poor.
You'll always be my love,
My soul mate forevermore.

I love you when you're happy
And when you're cranky too.
I love you more than all the stars
That surround the moon.

You're my love, my life.
You're my smiles and my laughter.
You're the beat to my heart…
My joy everafter.

Next To You

Hugging in the grass
Kissing on the swings
Texting during class
Sharing these feelings.
Looking in your eyes
With you looking into mine
Happiness that never dies
When we're together, we stop time.
We're alone together in this world
It's just you and me.
I'll always be your girl
Baby, can't you see?

One Thing… I Love You.

You were my first slow dance.
You were my first real date.
We did everything together
And you said you'd teach me to skate.

You cried with me for hours
You even wrote me a letter.
You gave me bouquets of roses.
You lips were soft as feathers.

I've kept everything
That reminds me of you
The cards, the clothes,
The matching shoes.

My shoes that matched yours
And the Louis Vuitton bag too.
The Smurf hats, the teddy bear,
All the memories of me and you.

The pictures in their frames,
The baby oil in my desk drawer.
These are but a few things,
There is so much more.

Your hoodie, your beanie,
Your Adidas jacket and pants.
A few more things I have,
That remind me of our romance.

'Fly Like A G6' and
'I ❤ Haters' shirts.
Reminder me of you
And how you took away my hurt.

Our initials that I painted.
Green and blue. C and A.
I still remember what I was wearing
When we met back in May.

The first time I saw you
At the Van Ness metro stop.
I had on a white cardigan, blue jeans
And my British flag tank top.

Then at the party,
With thunder and May showers.
I had on dark blue skinnies
And a tank top with pink flowers.

When we were in Dupont
Jeans, a white shirt, zebra print shoes.
You told me you loved me,
I should have said 'I love you too.'

It was never a crush,
At first sight it was love,
And since that day at the metro
You're the man I've been dreaming of.

Vroom

I jumped in my car
And followed my heart
Then I met you
And put it in park.

3's

On the twenty-fifth of May
In two-thousand-eleven
God gave me an Angel
Sent straight down from heaven.
Someone to always
Stand by my side.
Someone I can
Forever call mine.
A hand to hold
And lips to kiss.
So when I'm away
I'll have someone to miss.
I cherish you now
I cherished you then.
And if I had to choose,
I'd choose you again.
My one true love,
The one I can't live without.
You treated me right
And showed me what love was about.
Singing to me on the bus
Being lovey-dovey in front of friends.
I know for a fact,
That we'll never really end.
A tattoo is forever,
And you're getting our date.
This love wasn't a chance,
It happened by fate.

Heartbreak. Warfare.

"When you're dreaming with a broken heart, the waking up is the hardest part." –John Mayor

Blame It On Me

She knows that she wasn't all to blame,
It's just that her mom never felt the same.
She died when she said she was done,
It's a game she played well but wouldn't have won.

Epitaph of Lost Love

I never thought I'd say goodbye
I never knew how much I could cry
Or how much my chest could ache
Or how I'd nearly died at your wake.

I never thought my heart would crack
I just wish to bring you back.
Baby why did you have to leave?
Why can't this just be a dream?

Now that your time has finally stopped
Now that life has broken your clock
It's time I let go of our love.
Go with the other Angels above.

Epiphany

I hope one day you wake up
And you realise…
That you never fall in love
When you look into her eyes…
That she doesn't make you feel
The way you did around me
That you finally understand
Why we should be
Because I am me
And you are you
And we having a feeling
Of love that's true
But you left me alone
Left me here to cry
I'll never again fail
Cause you can't fail if you don't try.

Here Comes Goodbye

I don't want you as a mother
I don't want you as a friend
Even I know I'll always love you
Until the very end
I'll always reminisce about
The silly things we used to do
And I'll never forget the first memory
Of you saying, "I love you"
The way you held my hand so tight
And you loved my good and bad
You lied all the time and made me cry
But sometimes you were the only person I had
The sun doesn't shine
As bright as it used to be
The rain falls more often like my tears
Since the day you left me
I'll never forget the feeling
Of when my heart shattered
Mommy, I did all I could and tried my best
My best wasn't good enough, but that doesn't matter.

I Could Make Oceans With My Tears

I sit in utter silence,
Reminiscing of what was.
Trying to forget the pain,
Forget about your "love."

I throw the picture frame on the floor,
It skitters out of sight.
I let myself cry & cry
Cause I know our family wasn't right.

I hug my knees into my chest,
And let my head hang low.
I hear footsteps so I wipe the tears,
I can't let my feeling show.

My phone buzzes,
And there's your name.
My heart stops, I shed a tear,
And here comes the pain.

You promised you'd never leave me,
That you'd never walk away.
How hard is it to tell the truth?
Or believe what I say?
How hard is it to be happy
With what I've given you?
It's so hard for me to realise
With you lies are all I knew

I was closed,
But I opened up to you.
My brick walls were up,
But you tore your way through.

Not only did you lie to yourself,
But you also lied to me.
I can't believe I was blind,
And I couldn't really see...

I Stand Over Her Grave

I stand over her grave
And I remember what she used to be.
Always a hero, always brave,
And how she treated me.

Her name engraved in stone
Above the day that she died
When I found out I was alone
I broke down and cried.

The rain falls down
And I let the flowers go
I whisper, "I love you…"
That's all I needed her to know.

I Will Protect You

When I close my eyes
I tell myself it'll be alright…
That our family was wrong
That I should just move on

I remember your hands in mine
How with you I was always fine
How I never thought you'd leave
How I thought you'd always be my mommy.

I don't miss you when you're not here
I can't forget all of your fear.
I'll never be satisfied cause you're gone.
I want to know what I did wrong.

I was everything you wanted me to be
So why did you chose to leave me?
What does your man have that I have not?
All you guys ever do is fight.

Nothing about me has changed
Mommy, I'm still the same
So why does he get your heart
Why did you tear mine apart?

Walk Away…

When you're alone
And missing me.
Remember it was your decision
You chose to leave.

When he's in your arms
Sleeping and dreaming
Remember when you left
You left me grieving.

I grew up
And now I'm strong
I finally realized
I never did anything wrong.

You said I'd be okay
That you know I'll move on.
And yet you're the one
Who is calling me at dawn?

You're on your knees
Begging me
To take you back
I say leave.

You took my heart
Tore it to shreds
I spent months
Looking like I was dead.

As soon as I move on
You're ready to take me back?
I don't know what to do
I just know I'm not going back.

You're So Good To Me. Baby.

I tried so hard
But sorrow still follows me
I tried to make us happy
But I ended up in misery
I tried to be your everything
I honestly tried so hard
I did all that I could
I even gave you my heart
I told you it wasn't steel
That I had already begun to crack
You paid me no attention
And you broke my heart of glass
You've played with fire
From the very start
You just lit another match
To my paper heart.

Family Portrait

"In our family portrait we look pretty happy, let's play pretend, lets act like it comes naturally." –P!nk

Alone

I had my hair up
And my shoes laces done
I had on a funky t-shirt
I was ready to have some fun
You told me not to go
That here I should stay
You're scared I'd be speechless
But I know what to say
I got there on time
And I took my seat
Way in the back
In rows that were neat
One after one we stood
And presented what we had
It was my turn I stood alone
Just so I could present my dad

Brick Walls Can Break… Deal With It

I feel the heat of your body
Closing in on mine.
I feel the force of your swing,
You finally crossed the line.
I see my arms and face,
Colored black and blue.
I can't believe I still love you,
After all you've put me through.

The piercing screams of terror,
Haunt me in my sleep.
I sink to my knees,
As I watch you bleed and weep.
I sit up at night
And pray for a better day.
I rack my mind for words,
Only to find nothing to say.

I know I shouldn't feel like this,
I should hate you with all my heart,
But that's so hard to do,
When I have loved you from the start...

I can smell the alcohol,
As he sits there and lies.
Her cheeks are streaked with tears,
As she falls down and cries.
His fist hits her face,
Then there's a crack from her neck.
I pray to God she's still alive,
I don't really wanna check.

I reach out for you,
Put your hand in mine.
We can run away forever,
Run away from time.
But soon I'm out of dreams,
Back into reality.

I don't wanna wake up tomorrow,
Can't I live in this fantasy?

I know I shouldn't feel like this,
I should hate you with all my heart,
But that's so hard to do,
When I have loved you from the start...

Eating Tacks For Snacks

Mommy's body hits the floor.
Daddy's walking out the door.
From the little sores,
Comes liquid in a crimson colour.

The makeup smears as I cry.
I don't believe how much one man can lie.
I give up, I'm not going to try.
I look up and ask God why?

I scream and yell until it hurts.
I throw things and hit things, nothing works.
I hope you die, you damn jerk.
A slash of silver, and crimson spurts.

Daddy's always hitting
and Mommy doesn't care.
I have no one to love me.
No one is ever there.

Daddy left me long ago.
Mommy got around, put on a show.
She played it cool so I wouldn't know.
You may be good at acting, you're a bad liar though.

The babies are crying in the next room,
I'm hoping momma will be home soon.
Daddy yells, things go BOOM!
I feel a burn. Here comes doom.

Who says love is not a crime?
Daddy comes back, drunk outta his mind.
He says he doesn't like to see us cryin'
He won't do it again, I know he's lyin'.

Mira, Como Estoy Sufriendo

Mi mama es como un sube y baja,
Siempre hacia arriba o hacia abajo;
Sin poder equilibrarse.

Mi mama es como la lluvia,
Calmante para algunos, tediosa para otros;
Sin embargo, no puede satisfacer a todos.

Mi mama es como una zombi,
Muerta en el interior, sin embargo, arruinando mi vida;
Ataca y roba mi almoa.

Mi mama no es normal,
Ella te ama y despues te deja;
Cree en mí, me ha dejado.

Smiling A Crooked Smile

All she wants is a little love and affection.
All she needs is a little care and protection.
She's the girl with tears in her eyes.
She's the girl who sits alone and cries.

With a fire in her heart,
And the devil in her soul.
She feels her body breaking apart,
It all started with a little hole.

Bruises and welts down her back,
The pain brings her to the ground.
Here he comes. Here's the attack.
Her arms and legs tightly bound.

She screams and cries for help,
But no one hears her ask.
If you understood the pain she felt,
You'd have taken up the task.

She hears his footsteps down the hall,
She scrambles and tries to hide.
He comes in and throws her against the wall,
Her mom watches silently from behind.

She begs him to stop,
Says it's not her fault.
Her hits her and her bones pop
As her body lands on asphalt.

He says she's ugly and she's dumb,
That she's worthless white trash.
He beats her until she's numb,
Until she can't take it. There's a crash.

She wants her mom to care,
She wants her dad to leave.
Her mom is never there,

And now she's scared to breathe.

As he staggers in the door,
With alcohol on his breath.
He drops the beer bottle on the floor,
And she prays that tonight she won't meet death.

Make me a bird so I can fly,
Far, far away from here,
It never happened, she's alive,
But she lives every minute in constant fear.

Once again the police come,
And scare her really bad.
She thought that this madness was done,
She thought they would take her dad.

But they didn't take him out,
They left him there to stay.
So her mommy and daddy would shout,
Half the night and all day.

She wants friends to keep her safe,
She wants parents who love her.
She wants to be in a better place,
Or to live life in a blur.

All she wants is to be able to smile
And have someone who will hold her awhile.
Who won't hurt her or cause her pain.
Who will wipe away the tears that fall like rain.

F is For Friends

"Friends are like bras; there for support and always close to the heart." -Anonymous

Amores Como El Tuyo

La amistad es amor,
La amistad es vida.
La amistad son calidos rayos de sol,
Después de una tormenta.
La cura de nuestros miedos,
Y nuestra dolor.

La amistad es una toalla,
Que absorbe todas las lagrimas que lloras.
La amistad es la felicidad,
Después de un corazon roto.
La amistad es voodoo,
Que te revive duepués de morir.
La amistad es algo,
Que ted a un nuevo comienzo.

La amistad son la letra,
De la melodía de mi vida,
La amistad es la coreografia,
De un video musical.
La amistad es la mano,
Que controla un cuchillo.
La amistad es el sol de primavera,
Que sale y derrite la nieve.

La amistad es amor,
La amistad es vida.
La amistad son calidos rayos de sol,
Después de una tormenta.
La cura de nuestros miedos,
Y nuestra dolor.

E.A.V.M.

There are smiles in your eyes
But I can still see your pain
And your heart is a summer sky
No clouds, but it still rains

Love Me Until The End

As they walk down
This cold dirt path
They begin to forget
About the confusing past.
They know that
As long as they're together
All the pain and fear
Will get better.

Thank you for being my best friend.

No One Is Good Enough For You, Except Me!

It's been nine years,
Is that all?
How could something that felt like forever,
Be so small?

I've confided in you,
And soaked your shirts with tears.
We've had our differences,
But you've put up with me for years.

I ignored you. i left.
I told you to leave me be.
Through it all, you stayed by my side;
You never gave up on me.

I promise i'll love you,
Until the very end.
Being a homie, a lover,
Being your best friend.

There's An Angel Calling Me

You tell me you can't sing,
Yet you spend 20 minutes singing about me.
You don't believe you're gorgeous,
But you're the most gorgeous girl I've seen.
You tell me that you give up,
You just don't like it when you don't know.
You tell me that it doesn't hurt,
You just don't let your emotions show.
You tell me you're a bad friend,
But you're one of the best that I've known.
You tell me that you can't trust anyone,
But I'll always be by your side, you'll never be alone.

According To You

"This is real, this is me, it's exactly who I'm supposed to be." –Demi Lovato

I'm Your Soldier

I cover my mouth
Because I'm too afraid to scream.
I try not to close my eyes
Because I'm scared of my dreams.

Losing My Grip And Falling

The rabbit came and went,
He chased me down the hole.
I'm taking Alice's place,
Falling into Wonderland.
Walking down a path,
Meeting the two brothers.
They try their best to help,
But send me straight to hell.
The caterpillar smoking,
Doesn't turn into a butterfly.
No matter what I say he's mellow,
His tone won't change. He doesn't yell.
The cat hiding in the tree,
With nothing but his smiling showing.
Doesn't help me along the way,
He leaves me with a sarcastic goodbye.
The Mad man who has a hobby,
Of creating the best hats.
Isn't even a mad man,
He is the sanest of them all.
I eat the cake,
But it's poisoned.
I drink the liquid
But it's toxic.
I find the key,
Go through the door.
But all I see is haze,
Then the world is gone.
I meet the Queen of Hearts,
She is a very sweet lady.
I'm taking Alice's place,
It's happening all over again.
I'm falling down the hole,
Falling into Wonderland.

Me Vuelva Loca

Behind these big eyes
You can't see a past
Of heart ache
And family that didn't last.

Behind these blue eyes
No tears have been cried
For you.
It was kept inside.

Behind these beautiful eyes
Are images of what is gone.
Taken with the wind,
Images of what was done wrong

Behind these clear eyes
You find the real me.
Not the girl I am to you.
Not the girl I try to be.

Sabes Que Te Quiero, Con Todo El Corazon

Mi amor es más fuerte,
Que la fuerza del fuego violento.

Sólo hay una llave,
La llave de mi corazón,
Te adervtí que no la perdieras,
Fuiste tu quien la perdió.

Mi amor es más fuerte,
Que la fuerza del fuego violento.
Me enamore de ti,
Y mi corazón se rompió durante ese amor,
Lo recogiste,
Y lo volviste a tirar.

Mi amor es más fuerte,
Que la fuerza del fuego violento.
Te sigo amando,
Pero tú la amas a ella,
Todavía te extraño,
Más cuando sée que estas con ella.

Mi amor es más fuerte,
Que la fuerza del fuego violento.
Ya el fuego está muerto,
Muerto como yo.

Lloré por muchas horas.
Y ahora me estoy muriendo
De tristeza.

Todo eso por ti.
Por la persona que… yo amo.

This Is Me It's Not Who You Thought I'd Be

She's the one with the fake smile.
The one who was never a child.
The one that no one knows.
The one without ups, only lows.
The girl with tears in her eyes.
Who doesn't know truth, lives in lies.
The one who built up phony brick walls.
The one who crumbles and falls.
She's a prisoner in her own mind.
She was innocent, but she's still doing time.
The girl who has lost so many friends.
The girl who prays for a peaceful end.
Who can't wait till she finds love.
Who knows there are plans made above.
She let her past consume her.
She let's her life go by in a blur.
She doesn't want to see what's real.
She doesn't want to remember how to feel.
She loves the quiet, the sense of being alone.
She's hates the pain, but it's what she's known.
She doesn't know what to do with life.
She doesn't know if it's worth the fight.
She's stupid and weird.
She's an outcast and feared.
She's not who you think she is.
She's just someone's mistake of a kid.
She's a victim of abuse.
She's never let the real her lose.
She's afraid of what people will say.
She's afraid this will be her last day.
She's not the prettiest girl.
She's not the skinniest in the world.
She has a heart broken from attack.
This girl's life is a train off track.
The girl who is lost and won't be found.
The girl who tries to hide underground.
The girl who wishes you couldn't see her.
The girl who's voice is but a murmur.

The girl who was never given a chance.
The girl who was never given a second glance.
The girl who prays every night.
The girl who hates the morning light.
The girl who just told you her past.
The girl who you'll pass up fast.
The story just told is completely real.
She's wishes you'd understand how bad she feels.

Miscellaneous

"My best friend gave me the best advice, she said each day is a chance not a given right."
- Nickelback

Irony Poem of Tests

I stayed up all night
Studying for the test
I made sure I could answer right
So I'd do my very best.
I got my test and my pen
I wrote down my name
And the date and then,
I realised I couldn't answer the same.
All the studying the night before
Was a huge waste
I answered one question, not anymore,
And I got an Flunk not an Ace!

An Empty Room Can Be So Loud

The silence in this room
Is so very loud.
I'm so lonely
While I stand in this crowd.
I call out for you
But you never come
I wake up and realise
That we're done.

But I'm not going to cry
I'm not going to be sad
I'm going to smile at the memories
Of what we once had.
I'm going to remember
The way that I felt
When I was yours
And there was no one else.

Yes it hurts to know
That you're already gone.
Yes I do listen to
What used to be our song.
Yes I do still shed a tear
Every now & then.
But I quickly wipe them away
And hold my head high again.

I'm doing fine
I'm doing alright
I can finally sleep
Through the lonely nights.
But I don't mind the quiet
Or the empty space
Because I'm never fully alone
Your memory fills the place.

Autumn Air

As I walk through this little park
And breathe in the Autumn air,
I see families smiling and laughing,
And happiness is everywhere.

I walk through the piles of leaves
And watch couples walk by.
I listen as parent's console
A new borne as it cries.

The sun standing high
And the trees standing tall.
The colour of the trees are fading,
And people are sitting on the wall.

The farther I walk through the park,
The more smiles I see.
And I am so glad people are smiling.
This is what makes me happy.

Walking through a park.
Watching people laugh.
I look forward to a bright future.
And I dim the light of the past.

Blah Blah Justice Blah Blah

There is no more justice.
Nothing is ever fair.
You're called dumb and stupid,
Because of the colour of your hair.

If you're a woman you're weak.
If you're a man you have to be strong.
We believe only man and woman can love.
Why is man and man so wrong?

If you're not white you're believed to be lower.
It's always white people this. White people that.
You can only be pretty if you're skinny.
And you're ugly if you're fat.

Why can't we live in peace?
Why can't we love each other?
Why are we alone?
Why aren't we brothers?

Empowerment and Change

Every day it's always the same.
Get up.
Get ready.
Hide the pain.

Cover my eyes so you can't see the tears.
Of the past.
Of the present.
Of the future years.

But then I was saved.
He came.
He helped.
He made the change.

Every morning I wake up smiling.
It's sunny.
It's happy.
I'm not crying.

I frolic through the flowers he sent.
He won,
Me over.
Empowerment.

In The End It's Smiles and Tears

Life is like a roller coaster,
It goes up and down.
Life is like a circus,
There are always clowns.
Life is like gravity,
Always keeping you on the ground.
Life is like karma.
What goes around comes around.

Irony Poem of Tests

I stayed up all night
Studying for the test
I made sure I could answer right
So I'd do my very best.
I got my test and my pen
I wrote down my name
And the date and then,
I realised I couldn't answer the same.
All the studying the night before
Was a huge waste
I answered one question, not anymore,
And I got an Flunk not an Ace!

It's Time To Say It, Goodbye.

I take out the photo album
And my box of items
Everything that means something
Everything that has a memory

I spread it out on the floor
And look over it once
Pick up one thing
That shines brighter than the rest

A photo wrapped in gold lining
Covered by a dusty sheet of glass
With one swift gust of wind
Come back thousands of memories from the past.

Los Grandes Amores De Muchos Colores

La primavera está lejos,
Cuando los monstruos salen.

La primavera está lejos,
Cuando el festín se come.

La primavera está lejos,
Cuando Santa viene.

La primavera está lejos,
Cuando el año nuevo viene.

La primavera está lejos,
Cuando celebramos el amor.

La primavera está cerca,
Cuando nos vestimos de verde durante todo el día.

La primavera ha llegado,
En el 05 de mayo.

La primavera se ha ido,
Y lo perdermos por meses.

Entonces vamos a esperar,
A otra primavera.

Never A Right Time To Say Goodbye

When you say goodbye,
You're leaving for the last time.
You're pretty much saying
Out of sight, out of mind.

Super Star Baby

So when I'm a super star
Baby, look where you are
I'm up in front of the crowd
And they're screaming my name so loud
You'll be watching from afar
Cause baby I'm not your super star,

You let me go without a thought
Did you ever think that decision was wrong?
Do you ever wonder if I care?
Or what life would be like with me there?
Do you ever regret letting me go
If you do, I don't want to know…

Baby look at me
Baby, look what I've done!
Is this who you thought I'd be?
Do you still think I'm not fun?

So when I'm a super star
Baby, look where you are
I'm up in front of the crowd
And they're screaming my name so loud
You'll be watching from afar
Cause baby I'm not your super star,

I'll be singing so loud
That your thought is blocked out
I won't be looking for you
I'll be looking for someone new
I'm who I'm supposed to be,
Don't come back for me.

I was scared when I lost you
Like I was just another girl, nothing new
I'm sorry baby that I'm not good enough
To be everything you're dreaming of
But that doesn't matter, you were just a game
That I played so well I can't remember your name!

Baby look at me
Baby, look what I've done!
Is this who you thought I'd be?
Do you still think I'm not the one?

So when I'm a super star
Baby, look where you are
I'm up in front of the crowd
And they're screaming my name so loud
You'll be watching from afar
Cause baby I'm not your super star,

No! No! Noooooooooooooooooo!
I can't be with you anymore!
You want me back
But the night you left was our last…

Cause the table has finally turned
I guess you never learned
That what goes around comes around
And when something it's lost it's not found.

Tanka of Trees & Life

The tree limbs are like
Praying hands. Reaching up to
The heavens above
And asking for miracles.
The trees are our ancestors.

Tengo Un Sueño

Llegará el día, cuando nos podamos parar juntos,
Sin importar nuestro físico,
Sin importar de donde vengas.

Llegará el día, cuando las mujeres estén en control,
Vamos a gobernar el país,
Seremos nosotras quienes tomen las decisiones.

Llegará el día, cuando tu puedas ser tu,
No tendrás que preocuparte,
Sobre ser lastimado por otros.

Llegará el día, cuando las guerras se acaben,
Cuando podamos vivir en paz,
Y no necesitamos el dolor.

Llegará el día, se que vendrá.
Le rezamos a nuestros protectores.

Llegará el día.
Pero no sera pronto.

Two Roads Diverged Into A Single Wood

There may be one road
But there are two sides.
The choice you make either shortens
Or lengthens your stride.

Un Aguacera De Mayo

Mis sueños no son para mí misma solamente,
Mis sueños son por tí también.

Sueno que vivas en paz y amor, Y,
Que descurbras, que te amo…

Mis sueños no son para mí misma solamente,
Mis sueños también son para todo el mundo.

Sueno en que algún día paren las guerras. Y,
Que todos sepan, que no necesitamos violencia.

Mis sueños son para mí misma solamente,
Mis sueños no incluyen a nadie,

Porque todo que lo quiero,
No me quieren.

You Cry But Don't Tell Anyone

There is a fine line
Between the earth & sky.
It's even thinner
Between giving up and wanting to try.